I'M SORRY

I'm sorry : the art of
apology an   of

I'M SORRY

THE ART OF APOLOGY

AND THE GIFT OF FORGIVENESS

))) hatherleigh

Text Copyright © 2012 Hatherleigh Press

No part of this book may be reproduced, stored in a
retrieval system, or transmitted, in any form or by any
means, electronic or otherwise, without written permission
from the Publisher.

Hatherleigh Press is committed to preserving and protecting
the natural resources of the Earth. Environmentally
responsible and sustainable practices are embraced within
the company's mission statement.

Hatherleigh Press is a member of the Publishers Earth
Alliance, committed to preserving and protecting the
natural resources of the planet while developing a
sustainable business model for the book publishing industry.

Library of Congress Cataloging-in-Publication Data is
available upon request.
ISBN: 978-1-57826-413-1

I'm Sorry is available for bulk purchase, special promotions,
and premiums. For information on reselling and special
purchase opportunities, call 1-800-528-2550 and ask for the
Special Sales Manager.

10 9 8 7 6 5 4 3 2 1

Printed in the United States

CONTENTS

A NOTE FROM THE PUBLISHER

When I was 18, an important person in my life shared with me a page torn from *Reader's Digest*. On it was a simple quote, "An apology is a friendship preserver, an antidote for hatred, never a sign of weakness; it costs nothing but one's pride, always saves more than it costs, and is a device needed in every home".

That wisdom stuck with me through the years and, humbling as it may be to apologize to another, I came to find that the humility experienced is by far outweighed by the greater benefits of the act.

As you will discover in the following pages, apology and the hoped-for acknowledgement of forgiveness are powerful components of human growth and wholeness. In fact, letting go of past hurts and resentments through the act of forgiveness has a beneficial effect not only on our souls, but on our physical well-being as well.

We are fragile creatures, us humans—sensitive, reactive, vulnerable to pain and emotional distress. That is just the way we have been created. However, we are given the capacity to release ourselves and others and allow for healing through the process of contrition and resolution.

It is my hope that, in reading this book, you will gain greater encouragement to move forward and recognize the immense influence you can exert over your life and the world around you through the simple act of apology and the rewarding of forgiveness to others . . . and, at times, to yourself.

I'M
SORRY

The practice of peace and reconciliation is one of the most vital and artistic of human actions.

—Thich Nhat Hanh

INTRODUCTION

AT SOME POINT IN our lives, every one of us makes a mistake. Our mistake may offend, injure, or otherwise cause distress in a friend, loved one, family member, or co-worker. Similarly, each one of us will, at some point, feel that we have been wronged or slighted by the actions or words of someone else.

It is vital to our relationships that we learn how to free ourselves from our mistakes and from the anger we may feel towards someone who has hurt us. This is achieved through the cycle of apology and forgiveness. Whether you need to apologize or have received an apology, learning to let go is of the utmost importance. Otherwise, we risk engaging in fractured

Forgiveness is a virtue of the brave.

—INDIRA GANDHI

relationships, misusing our energy, and compromising our health.

This book will help you gain a solid understanding of what steps to take in order to make things right if you have offended someone and need to say "I'm sorry." The following pages will also shed some light on the ways in which those around you may have been offended, to help open your mind to their perspective so that you can apologize with genuine feeling. You will also learn why admitting a wrongdoing and asking for forgiveness—and granting forgiveness if you've been wronged—is the only way to move on to learn, grow, and ultimately experience all the benefits that your relationships have to offer.

THE MEANING OF
AN APOLOGY

According to the *Oxford Dictionary*, one of the definitions of "apology" is "a regretful acknowledgment of an offense or failure."

Forgiveness is like faith. You have to keep reviving it.

—MASON COOLEY

"Apology" can also be defined as "an assurance that no offense was intended" and "an explanation or defense." However, when it comes to doing what's best for our relationships, the first definition—"a regretful acknowledgment of an offense or failure"—is the most important. Above all else, an apology should be a genuine admission of a mistake. An apology can also include an assurance that we never meant to hurt another person. But placing too much emphasis on our good intentions, and failing to focus on the hurt our actions caused, can lead to resentment on the part of the person we are apologizing to. Similarly, although defending ourselves may be necessary in some specific cases, we shouldn't turn an apology into an explanation of our own point of view or perspective. The most important ingredient in any apology is the admission that we did something wrong. This is the first step towards reassuring someone that, although we may have temporarily overlooked their feelings when we made a mistake, our shortsightedness was just a slip-up.

Forgiveness is the answer to the child's dream of a miracle by which what is broken is made whole again, what is soiled is made clean again.

—DAG HAMMARSKJOLD

An apology serves to assure someone else that we have his or her best interests at heart and that we are committed to act in the best interest of the relationship.

THE MEANING OF FORGIVENESS

The word "forgive" is defined by the *Oxford Dictionary* as "to cease to feel angry or resentful towards; pardon (an offender or offense); remit or let off (a debt or debtor)." To forgive someone means we accept their apology for hurting us. It doesn't mean that we immediately cease to feel hurt, or that everything is suddenly okay. Forgiving does not necessarily mean forgetting. Instead, forgiving means we decide to deliberately let go of our negative feelings caused by the other person when they made a mistake. When we have been hurt, negative feelings like betrayal, anger, and resentment can come to the surface. Over time, if these feelings are not addressed, they can overwhelm us on both an emotional and

Forgiveness is the economy of the heart . . . forgiveness saves the expense of anger, the cost of hatred, the waste of spirits.

—HANNAH MORE

physical level. Granting forgiveness is truly a gift, not just to the person who has done wrong, but also to ourselves. Forgiveness allows us to let go of the past and move on.

DIFFERENT PERSPECTIVES ON FORGIVENESS

Forgiving provides us with the opportunity to let go of the past and move forward into the future with a new viewpoint and an open mind and heart. Seeking and obtaining forgiveness are important to maintaining healthy relationships and strong communities, as well as personal well-being. In fact, many religions and spiritual practices focus on it as a core teaching.

In Buddhism, forgiveness is essential for maintaining mental and emotional health. Buddhism encourages letting go of earthly possessions and reducing the power of the ego, often sought through the practice of meditation. When meditating on the meaning of life and what is truly important, it often

Forgiveness is the final form of love.

—REINHOLD NIEBUHR

becomes clear that what caused offense in the first place may actually be a petty concern. A person who is burdened by resentment cannot attain true enlightenment, so forgiveness is a vital tool for life within Buddhist teachings.

At the core of Christianity is the belief that God is able to forgive man of his sins if he confesses his wrongdoings. Although different forms of Christianity (such as Catholicism) place more emphasis on the importance of confession than others, some of the most important teachings of Jesus Christ center on the importance of forgiving those who have wronged us.

The holiest holiday in Judaism is Yom Kippur, which focuses on atonement and repentance. The holiday involves a day of fasting and prayer, when Jews meditate on mistakes they have made in the past year and seek forgiveness. As part of Yom Kippur, Jews ask forgiveness from God and also from each other. At the end of Yom Kippur, one is considered forgiven by God. This allows one to move on while also learning from one's mistakes.

Forgiveness is the giving, and so
the receiving, of life.

—GEORGE MACDONALD

THE IMPORTANCE OF FORGIVENESS

For Mental and Physical Health

Although forgiveness has been upheld as a key tenet in religious beliefs for thousands of years, it wasn't until the late 20th century that science began to explore the effects of forgiveness on the mind and body. Over time, studies have shown that people who forgive are happier and more physically healthy than people who continue to be angry, resentful, or vengeful. When we are angry with someone else, our immune systems are weakened. In contrast, forgiving someone allows us to let go of negative feelings and makes us less prone to illness. In fact, scientific data proves that even thinking about forgiving someone else can lead to improvements in cardiovascular and nervous system functioning. Forgiveness also leads to a sharp reduction in stress and the physical manifestations of stress. The health benefits go beyond physical health,

Forgiveness is the key to action and freedom.

—HANNAH ARENDT

too. We now know that people who forgive are also more self-confident and positive about the future, and have a better outlook on life in general.

Studies have also shown that, although some people are more prone to being forgiving than others, anyone can learn how to forgive. As Dr. Everett L. Worthington, Jr., PhD, the Campaign Executive Director of A Campaign for Forgiveness Research, states, "Forgiveness is both a decision and a real change in emotional experience. That change in emotion is related to better mental and physical health."

No matter what hurt we have suffered or whether we have been able to forgive in the past, each one of us can learn how to forgive, and open the door to improved health on both a physical and emotional level.

Whether you picked up this book seeking to forgive or to be forgiven, or if you are just looking for some guidance as you navigate the many relationships in your life, *I'm Sorry* will be a helpful tool. The process of forgiveness, whether we have been hurt or

Forgiveness is the remission of sins. For it is by this that what has been lost, and was found, is saved from being lost again.

—Saint Augustine

have hurt someone else, is a difficult one, but it presents the opportunity for us to learn, grow, and ultimately lead better lives. Let this book open a door in your heart to greater love and understanding towards others as well as yourself and start you on the path towards a richer, more meaningful life.

The secret of forgiving everything
is to understand nothing.

—George Bernard Shaw

PART I

THE ART OF APOLOGY

WHEN TO SAY YOU'RE SORRY:

Common Mistakes at Home,

Among Friends, and in the Workplace

Forgotten is forgiven.

—F. SCOTT FITZGERALD

APOLOGIZING IS HARD. When we experience this feeling, the first step is to explore *why* apologizing seems so challenging. Maybe we feel somehow resentful that we have to ask someone else for something (in this case, his or her pardon). Or the situation might be complicated and we feel we are owed an apology, too. (In this case, we may refuse to apologize because we want the other person to do so first.) Maybe we simply view the act of asking for an apology as a sign of weakness.

In cases like these, we should remember that taking the initiative to say "I'm sorry" is, in fact, a sign of strength. Coming face to face with our own feelings is also an opportunity for improvement that can lead to personal growth.

The lesson here is that the first step towards an apology is to let go of any feelings

Lord, make me an instrument of your peace; where there is hatred, let me sow love; where there is injury, pardon; where there is doubt, faith; where there is despair, hope; where there is darkness, light; and where there is sadness, joy.

—FRANCIS OF ASSISI

of superiority, resentment, or stubbornness. Only then can we tap into the power of the forgiveness cycle, and allow ourselves to get one step closer towards being truly free.

Apologizing isn't easy. But be sure to focus on how important it is to resolve conflict; if a situation is not addressed, there is the chance that relationships will erode over time. Learning to apologize, and understanding the process of being forgiven, is a powerful tool for moving on from the past and making your relationships stronger. When you apologize, you are asserting your belief in the importance of your relationships. Applaud yourself for your commitment to the people you know and love and acknowledge your courage in apologizing.

WHAT IS A
TRUE APOLOGY?

A true apology goes beyond simply saying, "I'm sorry." Although those are powerful words, a

Genuine forgiveness does not deny anger but faces it head-on.

—ALICE DUER MILLER

real apology consists of much more. Much in the same way that a wound takes time to heal, a person whose feelings have been hurt requires more than just the words "I'm sorry" to move on. A good apology seeks to repair the damage caused, and to lay the groundwork for preventing future transgressions by opening up the door to change; along with an admission of error may come the realization that patterns of behavior need to change over the long-term. A good apology can encourage communication that extends beyond what was done wrong. This makes an apology a valuable means to learn more about someone else and strengthen the relationship.

An apology should contain the elements necessary to heal the hurt you caused. This means saying what you have to say, and then taking the time to allow the other person to speak. Try to understand the other person's viewpoint to the best of your ability, and provide suggestions for ways to prevent the same mistake from happening again.

How does one know if she has forgiven? You tend to feel sorrow over the circumstance instead of rage, you tend to feel sorry for the person rather than angry with him. You tend to have nothing left to say about it all.

—CLARISSA PINKOLA ESTÉS

When apologizing, be sure that you:

- Genuinely state "I'm sorry" and admit wrongdoing.
- Listen to the other person's viewpoint. Discuss ways to prevent the mistake from happening again.
- Ask if you can do anything to make amends. Actions can speak volumes.

COMMON MISTAKES
In the Workplace, Among Friends, and at Home

All of us make mistakes. Sometimes, our mistakes directly affect and even hurt someone else. We may make a mistake by sending a pointed e-mail or text message. We may presume we know what's best for someone else, and offend by offering misplaced advice. We may overstep our boundaries and tell someone else what to do in an insensitive manner. Often, if we aren't aware of the effect of our actions, one mistake can lead to another. For

How unhappy is he who cannot forgive himself.

—Publilius Syrus

example, rushing through the day and failing to give someone else the attention they deserve can wound a family member. If we continue to be rushed in our actions as the day goes on, we can also cause a colleague to feel slighted. Slip-ups can occur in our personal lives at home or among friends, or in our professional lives in the workplace.

WE TRY TO DO TOO MUCH

Our lives today are moving faster than ever before. As a result, we are often rushing to keep up in order to finish everything we feel we need to accomplish. The stress of having too much to do in too little time can affect our relationships. We may show up late to a meeting, cut off a friend when they are speaking, or do a less-than-perfect job in the office in order to complete all the things on our to-do list. Even worse, when we are talking fast, working fast, or trying to get out the door, we can sometimes say something hurtful, without even realizing it. Slowing down enough to recognize what is truly important—the

Humanity is never so beautiful as when praying for forgiveness, or else forgiving another.

—JEAN PAUL RICHTER

people around us—is the key to preventing further injury. Taking the time to rectify the situation is important for us and the people we care about.

A CASE OF MISCOMMUNICATION

Despite having several ways to be in touch at our fingertips, miscommunication is still common in this day and age. Part of the reason for this is that, oftentimes, we simply don't speak in person or over the phone. Rather, we rely on text messages or e-mails, which are impersonal means of communicating and can often be misunderstood. Without the context of someone's facial expression or the sound of their voice, some messages can come across as harsh or demanding. If we have to turn someone down because we are too busy to meet up, doing so through e-mail or text can come across as insensitive or seem like rejection. This may occur in the office, between friends, or at home. Although a mistake like this seems small, it is important to address how we may have injured someone so that we

I can forgive, but I cannot forget, is only another way of saying, I will not forgive. Forgiveness ought to be like a cancelled note—torn in two, and burned up, so that it never can be shown against one.

—HENRY WARD BEECHER

can prevent it from happening again and so that our future correspondence doesn't have negative overtones.

SHORTER ATTENTION SPANS

There are so many demands on our time and attention, coming at us from e-mail, text messages, and cell phones that this can influence how we relate to others. For example, we may not give someone the attention they deserve when they are speaking to us in the office, at home, or when we are out with friends, which can be hurtful. Our compromised attention spans may prevent us from recognizing that we've hurt someone else. Learning to pay attention to how our actions affect others is vital.

OVERSTEPPING OUR BOUNDARIES

Anytime anyone else shares worries, problems, or concerns, it is tempting to go beyond just listening and begin to offer advice. Sometimes, our words can be helpful. Other times, our

With forgiveness, your victim identity dissolves, and your true power emerges—the power of presence. Instead of blaming the darkness you bring in the light.

—ECKHART TOLLE

advice can transform from a helpful sugges-
tion to an expression of our opinion about the
way someone else is living his life or conduct-
ing himself at home or at work. It's important
for us to remember that we never truly know
what things are like for someone else and, as
such, it isn't our place to tell someone how to
live. Furthermore, if we've made the mistake
of overstepping our boundaries, it's important that we apologize to reassure our friend,
family member, or co-worker that we can be
a trusted confidant in the future and that we
don't judge them.

SAYING SOMETHING HURTFUL

Despite our best intentions, if we are stressed,
overtired, or even feeling hurt from something
someone has said to us, we can let something
slip that is hurtful to someone else. Depending
on how strong our words are, we can either
cause a minor case of hurt feelings or, in the
worst case scenario, cause damage to a relationship. Apologizing for what we said is key
if we want to maintain a friendship, healthy

It is very easy to forgive others their mistakes; it takes more grit and gumption to forgive them for having witnessed your own.

—JESSAMYN WEST

family relationship, or working relationship. Saying something that wounds someone else is never justifiable, and it will help our own sense of self to acknowledge our error through an apology.

SIMPLY FORGETTING

It is inevitable that, with all we have on our plates today—from managing work and home life, to other daily duties and errands—we will inadvertently forget to get back to someone or do something we had promised. We may neglect to respond to an e-mail at work in a timely fashion, or forget to return a friend's phone call. Although these are innocent and understandable mistakes, feeling forgotten can, unfortunately, wound as much as an insult or other hurtful act. An apology is an important tool for reminding someone that we are sorry for our oversight, and that he is still in our thoughts, even if our actions may have given a negative impression.

Life is an adventure in forgiveness.

—Norman Cousins

MAKING ASSUMPTIONS

If we have known someone for some time, we may assume that we know how she thinks or feels. In the workplace, this can lead to speaking on her behalf, or making a decision without her in the room under the assumption that she would agree with us. At home, we may plan a family event without asking our spouse or children what they think. If we are meeting up with a friend or friends, we may make a decision about where to meet without consulting with them. It is always wise to ask someone what they really think before taking action. If we neglect to do so, it is important to apologize in order to assure that person that she is heard and appreciated and that her opinion always counts.

A DIFFERENCE OF OPINION

We won't always agree with someone else, even if it's someone close to us. Whether it's as simple as conflicting agendas, or as complicated as opposing viewpoints on weighty issues,

Mistakes are always forgivable,
if one has the courage to admit
them.

—BRUCE LEE

we have to accept that we may reach a point where our plans or beliefs simply differ from someone else's. In the workplace, this can cause problems if one person's viewpoint leads to change, while another's is ignored. At home, arguments that start out friendly can lead to hurt feelings, and we may feel especially slighted when we discover that what we thought we knew about someone turns out to be untrue. Among friends, it can feel like a betrayal if someone with whom we have a lot in common doesn't agree with us. Although we don't necessarily have to apologize for our own personal viewpoints, we should apologize to someone if we express our viewpoints in a way that is offensive or abrasive.

NOT STANDING BY OUR WORD

Sometimes, we make a promise to someone else and neglect to come through. The promise can be something as simple as saying we'll do something for a family member, or telling a friend we will follow-up with information we had promised. In the workplace, we may say

My desire is to be a forgiving, non-judgmental person.

—JANINE TURNER

we'll get to a task, then fail to do so; this kind of mistake can have serious repercussions if we fail to meet a deadline. Recognizing when we have neglected to come through after we said we would, and then rectifying the situation, is of paramount importance if we don't want people to form negative judgments about who we are. We should do everything we can to make up for the mistake and prove that we can be relied upon and that our word can be trusted.

Never forget the three powerful resources you always have available to you: love, prayer, and forgiveness.

—H. JACKSON BROWN, JR.

ALL OF US make mistakes; we are only human. Sometimes our mistakes may be obvious to us and the person we injured. Other times, we may not realize we have hurt someone until they let us know. Either way, having a solid understanding of how our actions can affect others, and a clear perspective on how someone else may feel, is the first step towards making an apology. Then, we are prepared to go to someone else and ask for his or her forgiveness in the most effective way possible. The reward is a repaired relationship, a chance for personal growth, and the promise of a brighter future with those close to us.

One forgives to the degree that one loves.

—FRANCOIS DE LA
ROCHEFOUCAULD

PART II

THE GIFT OF
FORGIVENESS

HOW TO SHOW YOU'RE SORRY:

The Best Ways to Apologize at Home,

Among Friends, and in the Workplace

People can be more forgiving than you can imagine. But you have to forgive yourself. Let go of what's bitter and move on.

—BILL COSBY

A T SOME POINT IN our lives, each one of us will seek forgiveness for something we have done wrong. When we ask for forgiveness, we should remember what it was like when others came to us for the same thing. What elements of another person's apology meant the most to us? Sometimes heartfelt words can be enough; other times a special gesture, like a gift or a walk together, are necessary to restore our trust and reaffirm the bond between us. Were there portions of the apology that offended or somehow made us feel worse? If an individual who is apologizing spends too much time defending their position or trying to justify what they did, it can make us feel cheated or disregarded. Keep these things in mind when you go to another person to seek their forgiveness.

The ineffable joy of forgiving and being forgiven forms an ecstasy that might well arouse the envy of the gods.

—ELBERT HUBBARD

WHAT DOES IT MEAN
TO TRULY FORGIVE?

Forgiving someone else does not necessarily mean that we come to agree with the person who has wronged us. On the contrary, we have the right to say, "I wish you hadn't done that." Forgiveness does not wipe the slate clean or start everything anew. Instead, forgiveness acknowledges a mistake and lets go of negative feelings. In this way, forgiving someone reasserts our belief in them and our commitment to the relationship. We learn to see past our hurt feelings and, in this way, get one step closer to truly seeing someone else for who they are—flaws and all.

At its core, forgiveness is the decision to move on and move forward. Sometimes, forgiveness is complicated. We may have to forgive without any apology because the person who wronged us is no longer in our life. Or, we may simply be unable to ask for an apology if our hurt feelings are directed toward a group

The practice of forgiveness is our most important contribution to the healing of the world.

—MARIANNE WILLIAMSON

of individuals or an institution. We may even have to forgive ourselves for things we did to others or to our own person.

Forgiveness can be hard. Learning to see past our own hurt takes real effort. We can sometimes be so fixated on being right, or getting justice, that we stubbornly refuse to see past the situation. Unfortunately, this viewpoint only binds us. We are just as restricted by our own anger, rightful though it may be, as by anything else. Learning to let go is the only way forward.

HOW TO APOLOGIZE FOR COMMON MISTAKES
In the Workplace, Among Friends, and at Home

Although we may make the same types of mistakes in different situations, ways to apologize vary widely depending on whom we are apologizing to. For those we know best, an apology may include words of love and

The weak can never forgive.
Forgiveness is the attribute of the
strong.

—MAHATMA GANDHI

appreciation or a special gift or promise. For co-workers, however, a formal conversation is more appropriate and, depending on the type of error, other individuals in the office may also be involved. In the office, it's especially important that you not only apologize for your slip-up, but also make the effort to set things right. Otherwise, other people may end up having to work harder to correct your mistakes, causing resentment. Learning the best way to apologize is the first step to resolving any conflict and moving forward.

WE TRY TO DO TOO MUCH:
Ways to make it right

. . . in the workplace
If you show up late to a meeting, whether the meeting is with a group of people or an individual, go beyond just saying "I'm sorry" after you enter the room. Take action to truly express your regret. After the meeting, walk over to a co-worker's office or send an e-mail to apologize and assure your colleagues that

There is no love without forgiveness, and there is no forgiveness without love.

—Bryant H. McGill

you will make every effort to prevent the situation from happening again.

. . . *with friends*

In a situation where we may have been pressed for time and neglected a friend, it is important to do everything we can to reassure them that we care. If a friend feels slighted by your tardiness or rushed manner, start by genuinely saying "I'm sorry" rather than recounting a list of all the things you have to do as a way to explain your actions. It is important to keep the focus on her feelings, rather than focusing on your schedule. Then, ask your friend if she has any ideas about how you can either make it up to her or prevent the same thing from happening again.

. . . *at home*

Trying to get everything done in order to keep a household running is a huge challenge. But don't forget that the end goal is not a picture-perfect home. Rather, it is to create an environment where each person in the family feels acknowledged and loved. If you are caught up

To err is human; to forgive, divine.

—ALEXANDER POPE

in a web of to-dos and are always rushing, set aside time to sit with your family and apologize directly to anyone whose feelings you think may have been hurt. Then, ask everyone in the family to commit to making time for each other as much as possible. This will minimize the chances that someone will feel hurt again, and will provide you with the support you need to slow down a bit.

A CASE OF MISCOMMUNICATION:
Ways to make it right

. . . *in the workplace*

If you sent an e-mail that was misconstrued, make a point of walking over to your co-worker's office and apologizing. During your apology, you can state what it is that you intended to communicate, but be careful not to give excuses for your behavior. Be sure to take the time to ask them exactly why they felt slighted, and ask for their tips on how to prevent mistakes like this in the future. Say, "Thank you for taking the time to listen to

To forgive is to set a prisoner free and discover that the prisoner was you.

—LEWIS B. SMEDES

me, I'm so glad we've gotten some clarity on this matter."

. . . with friends

A friend who received an e-mail, phone call, or other message from you that hurt him will probably need more than just a brief written apology. Back up your "I'm sorry" with a positive statement that reaffirms his important role in your life. Reiterate how sorry you are, and ask him to please let you know if he'd like to meet up in person to talk; let him know it would be your pleasure and that, either way, you look forward to seeing him again soon.

. . . at home

In situations of miscommunication among family members, special care is required when apologizing. The apology should express what was really intended by the original message, for purposes of clarity. But be careful not to use that as an excuse or neglect to express regret for offending your spouse or child. In cases like this, who is right or wrong isn't important; what's important is the other

To understand is to forgive, even oneself.

—ALEXANDER CHASE

person's feelings. Be sure to take the time to ask how your communication was misconstrued, and apologize for the pain you may have caused the other person. ·

SHORTER ATTENTION SPANS:
Ways to make it right

. . . in the workplace

Not giving a co-worker (or co-workers) the attention that's required can have consequences which go beyond offending someone. If your lack of attention caused an oversight that disrupted workflow and affected someone else, be sure to find the problem and do what you can to make it right. Also apologize to the individual to whom you didn't give enough of your focus. If you feel that your attention span is constantly being compromised, you may have to propose that, in the future, you set aside the time to meet with someone in a specific place, such as her office (with her phone turned off and e-mail minimized) or a conference room. This will ensure that your conversation is distraction-free.

When you forgive, you in no way change the past—but you sure do change the future.

—BERNARD MELTZER

. . . with friends

Failing to give a friend the attention they deserve can be especially wounding. If we don't listen carefully, we may miss out on an important detail or story. When this is mentioned later and we don't acknowledge it, our friend can feel as if they don't matter. If you offend someone due to your compromised attention span, be sure to apologize to them in person. As part of the apology, consider pledging not to check your cell phone the next time you meet in person, or ask her if she has other ideas to prevent a future slight. If you find yourself apologizing for this type of mistake often, consider the possibility that your schedule is simply too packed for frequent socializing. If this is the case, carefully explain to your friend that the quality of your time together is more important than the quantity, and that your absence in the coming weeks will be balanced by a longer, one-on-one get-together once your workload lightens up.

You will know that forgiveness
has begun when you recall those
who hurt you and feel the power to
wish them well.

—LEWIS B. SMEDES

. . . at home

It can be hard to juggle priorities and give our spouse or children the attention they deserve. The household can often be a busy and hectic environment, with chores competing for our attention in every room. If a family member feels they weren't acknowledged, it's especially important to take the time to apologize with sincerity. Look the person in the eyes when you speak. To prevent hurt feelings in the future, try saying something like, "I am washing the dishes while you're talking, but I want you to know I am listening," or, "I'm sorry I can't give you the attention you deserve while we are on our way to school. I'd love it if we could talk about this later."

OVERSTEPPING OUR BOUNDARIES:
Ways to make it right

. . . in the workplace

Giving more advice than we should to a colleague about how to do her job can be especially harmful. This is true not only because we may offend someone, but also because

A stiff apology is a second insult ... The injured party does not want to be compensated because he has been wronged; he wants to be healed because he has been hurt.

—GILBERT K. CHESTERTON

(unless we are in a managerial or supervisory role) our advice can in fact directly contradict that person's official duties. If you say too much regarding someone else's job, you should include in your apology an acknowledgment that what you did was wrong and promise to refrain from doing that again. If your advice led someone to do something that was later determined to be outside of her role and she faced repercussions, offer to do what you can to right the wrong.

. . . with friends

A friendship is a relationship built on trust. Overstepping our boundaries and telling someone we care about what to do can be especially hurtful because it can come across as being judgmental. If a friend is upset by your words, take the time to explain that you were trying to give advice and, although your intentions may have been honorable, your behavior was inappropriate. Ask for your friend's feedback on how to address the situation in the future with something like, "What do you think is the best kind of advice I can give to you?" You can

An apology is the superglue of life.
It can repair just about anything.

—LYNN JOHNSTON

even ask, "In the future, would you prefer that I simply listen to your problems, rather than offer my advice?" You may discover that what your friend really needs is someone to listen and a shoulder to lean on. If you ask specifically, "What exactly about my words or advice upset you?" you may create an opportunity to learn more about your friend and reach a deeper level of mutual understanding.

. . . *at home*

At home, parents are often the ones who give advice or guidance to children. Even though years worth of experience certainly offer a valuable perspective, giving too much advice can sometimes communicate that we don't trust our child to act on his own. In your apology, acknowledge that your guidance was a bit heavy-handed and reiterate that you trust your children to make the right decision by themselves. Sharing advice with a spouse can sometimes come across as patronizing or dismissive of the other person's viewpoint if words of guidance aren't delivered correctly. When apologizing to your husband or wife,

Any fool can criticize, condemn, and complain but it takes character and self control to be understanding and forgiving.

—DALE CARNEGIE

take the time to make it clear that you weren't trying to live his or her life for them, or impose your own will. Ask, "Is there a better way that I can phrase my advice in the future?" Also state, "My primary goal is to help you because I love you. If you prefer that I help you by letting you choose your own path, I will understand."

SAYING SOMETHING HURTFUL:
Ways to make it right

. . . in the workplace

Harsh words in the workplace can fracture relationships and compromise future endeavors. The nature of your apology to a colleague will depend upon how severe your words were, and whether they were personal or work-related. If your offense was severe, you may want to ask a Human Resources representative for help to ensure that your apology includes all the elements necessary to pave the way towards reconciliation. If your words were not so wounding, asking another colleague for their perspective before you apologize

Apology is a lovely perfume; it can transform the clumsiest moment into a gracious gift.

—MARGARET LEE RUNBECK

might help; but be sure to avoid using your colleague to take your side. Instead, ask him what he thinks would be the most effective way to apologize.

. . . *with friends*

Saying something hurtful to a friend is a mistake that should be rectified as soon as possible. Letting time pass either because we don't want to deal with the situation, or because we are stubbornly waiting for the other person to apologize—can just cause the wound to deepen. On the other hand, if your words were especially rough, it may be wise to give your friend some time to cool down. When you reach out to her, start by saying, "I'm so sorry my words hurt you. You mean so much to me." If she speaks with anger in response, try saying, "I know you're upset with me but I'd really appreciate it if we could focus on communicating with respect and work on healing our relationship."

He who is devoid of the power
to forgive, is devoid of the power
to love.

—MARTIN LUTHER KING, JR.

. . . at home

It is particularly challenging when strong words are exchanged at home because we share the same living space. Among spouses, the time required to cool off may mean one of you has to leave the house for a time. If you upset your child, allow him to go to his room or another familiar space right away, but seek them out shortly after to say you're sorry. Making the effort to apologize quickly should be followed up with small, kind actions throughout the week that show you're really sorry.

SIMPLY FORGETTING:
Ways to make it right

. . . in the workplace

If you forgot to get back to someone at work, take the time to walk over to his or her workspace and apologize. Then, do what you can to bring them on board for the project at hand. Your actions will help prevent hurt feelings in the future and will add another valuable contributor to the team. If you feel

To forgive is indeed the best form of self-interest since anger, resentment, and revenge are corrosive of that "summum bonum," the greatest good.

—DESMOND TUTU

it is appropriate, you can go one step further and ask your colleague if he feels there was another time or place that his objectives were forgotten. If it is something that happens repeatedly, put systems in place (such as e-mail reminders or weekly check-ins) to prevent it from happening again.

. . . *with friends*

If you forget to catch up with a friend, returning a phone call or sending an e-mail reply may not be enough; his feelings have already been hurt, and he may feel mistrustful of you. Try sending a handwritten note or set up a date for coffee or to take a walk. This will help re-establish yourself in that person's mind as someone who really is there for him. Then, he will be able to fully understand that you really did make a mistake in neglecting to be in touch right away and that, in truth, he is never truly forgotten.

. . . *at home*

If we forget to do something small, like run an errand or accomplish another task, the

Let us forgive each other—only then will we live in peace.

—Leo Nikolaevich Tolstoy

simplest, and most powerful, form of apology can be doing what we said we'd do. If it's too late, be sure that the first thing you say when you apologize is, "I'm sorry I forgot to do that for you." Then, you can explain that the task simply slipped your mind and that you didn't intend to cause harm. The most important element of the apology is that you focus on the other person's feelings. Finally, ask your spouse or family member if they have any suggestions for helping you to stay on track in the future. If your schedule is simply too overloaded and your mistake is understandable, team up as a family to find a solution.

MAKING ASSUMPTIONS:
Ways to make it right

. . . in the workplace

If you made a decision on a colleague's behalf that affected her workload in the long-term, an apology should take into account reasons why you may have thought it best to speak for her. Were you trying to save time? This is a legitimate reason for your actions, but your

Love is an act of endless forgiveness, a tender look which becomes a habit.

—PETER USTINOV

apology should nonetheless acknowledge their feelings and contain an assertion that you won't do that again. Speaking for someone else can seem disrespectful, and you want to be sure it's clear that this is not what you meant.

. . . with friends

The best way to apologize for making an assumption about a friend's opinion depends on what we've done. If we took a guess at a place a friend would like to eat, only to discover that they didn't like the cuisine or that it was too expensive, the matter can quickly become complicated if our friend doesn't speak out. If you notice that a friend seems especially distant, it's a good idea to ask what you may have done to upset them. If they try to brush off your actions, be sure to say, "Wait, you're right. I made an assumption about what you wanted and acted on that. I should have asked you first before making a decision." This will lay the groundwork for better communication in the future and will help your friend feel heard.

When a deep injury is done us, we never recover until we forgive.

—ALAN PATON

. . . at home

Sometimes it's just impossible to make a decision about the family with everyone in the room. Other times, we may simply decide without asking anyone else in order to simplify our day. Regardless, we need to be sure to take the time to apologize for our actions. Assuming that we know what is better for a family member can make them feel small and disregarded. When you apologize, try not to defend your actions. Instead, acknowledge that you are sorry for making the decision without them, and ask how you can make it right. If necessary, you may have to change your plan. If that's not possible, offer to set aside a night to do what the other person wants. Your actions will make it clear that their opinion does count and they will feel acknowledged and gratified.

We achieve inner health only through forgiveness—the forgiveness not only of others but also of ourselves.

—JOSHUA LOTH LIEBMAN

A DIFFERENCE OF OPINION:
Ways to make it right

. . . *in the workplace*

Depending on what was said in the office, you may need to have a Human Resources representative or a senior staff member involved when making your apology. This will ensure that the issue goes on record as having been addressed. However, if your slip-up was not extreme, reaching out to a colleague and asking if you can meet up outside of the office to chat can be a meaningful gesture. When you speak, avoid defending your viewpoint or starting another disagreement. Instead, sincerely state that you are sorry your differences of opinion caused your co-worker to feel slighted. Even if you don't entirely agree in the future, your words will show that you value your colleague's well-being and harmony in the workplace more than being right.

Those free from resentful
thoughts surely find peace.

—BUDDHA

. . . with friends

Sometimes we expect that our friends will always agree with us. When this doesn't turn out to be true, we can become confused in the heat of the moment and may express ourselves more forcefully, inadvertently causing injury. If this happens, it's important to let your friend know that, above all else, the friendship is your priority. Apologize to her for your strong words and give her the chance to speak her mind. If you still don't agree, say, "I respect you for sharing your opinion. I'm glad we both have strong beliefs and that we share the courage to express them. Let's agree to respect each other's opinions even if we don't agree about the topic at hand." Then, ask if you can make a plan to go out together and let her choose where to go. Stepping aside to let your friend make the decision will show that you don't always have to be right and that the bond you share is paramount.

Sincere forgiveness isn't colored with expectations that the other person apologize or change. Don't worry whether or not they finally understand you. Love them and release them. Life feeds back truth to people in its own way and time.

—SARA PADDISON

. . . at home

Sometimes we forget that, although we are a family, we don't always share the same viewpoint. This may seem odd, but having different perspectives can actually enrich our time together—as long as you take the initiative to apologize to someone if you upset them when you shared your opinion. If you were rude or overly opinionated when you spoke to your family member, apologize for expressing yourself so forcefully. Let him know that you value his opinion and that you overstepped your bounds. Give him time to express his side of things if he didn't have a chance to do so earlier. (If necessary, you can do this during a family meal so that he feels truly heard by everyone.) Let him know that no matter what your opinions may be, what's most important is your love and respect for one another. If things still seem fractured, consider allowing someone from outside the family to come to the table. Sometimes all that's needed is a calm, objective viewpoint to restore order.

Forgiveness is a funny thing. It warms the heart and cools the sting.

—WILLIAM ARTHUR WARD

NOT STANDING BY OUR WORD:
Ways to make it right

... in the workplace

Neglecting to come through in the office can be especially problematic. If you didn't accomplish a task you said you would do and someone else had to make up the work for you, it's imperative that you apologize in person. In order to show that you are truly sorry and that you respect the other person's time, send her an e-mail asking when you can stop by to speak with her, rather than dropping in on her when she's busy. When you meet with her, sit down and look her in the eyes and give her a sincere apology. Tell her you promise not to make the same mistake again and that you will do what you can to regain her trust. If she did work on your behalf, consider saying, "I really appreciate the extra work you did. Is there some way I can help to lighten your workload, as a sign of my appreciation?"

Mutual forgiveness of each vice,
Such are the Gates of Paradise.

—WILLIAM BLAKE

. . . with friends

Coming through when we say we will is one of the ways we build trust and establish intimacy with those closest to us. When we drop the ball, we risk setting our friendship back. When you apologize to a friend for letting them down, it is important that you offer them a genuine admission of guilt. Don't offer excuses or explanations; instead, focus on their hurt feelings. Say, "I let you down. I'm so sorry. How can I make it up to you?" Be sure to let them know how important your friendship is to you, and that you are committed to strengthening the bond of trust you share. Last and not least, if it's not too late for you to follow through, do what you promised. Actions can speak louder than words.

. . . at home

Among family, failing to come through can cause major resentment in our spouse or children. In a family, everyone trusts everyone else to stand by what they say they would do; this helps the family work together in good times and bad. If you are a parent and you let

To be social is to be forgiving.

—ROBERT FROST

your child down, be sure they know that you understand there is no excuse for this. If you let down your spouse, make it clear that your mistake is uncalled for and that you are whole-heartedly sorry. Take the time to ask your wife or husband how your actions made them feel. This will allow them to calm down and release their feelings of resentment. Even if their words are hard to hear, know that their feedback will help establish a better pathway for the two of you in the future.

May I tell you why it seems to me
a good thing for us to remember
wrong that has been done to us?
That we may forgive it.

—CHARLES DICKENS

Apologizing takes courage, but the rewards of an apology are many. The strength an apology lends to a relationship, whether in the workplace, amongst friends, or in a family, provides benefits that last a lifetime. We can also learn more about ourselves and our fears and weaknesses when we apologize.

The process of forgiveness is also a challenging one. But striving to get to a place where we can forgive someone will not only expand our mind and heart and allow us to fully love others, but will also free us so that we can live the best lives possible. Apologizing and forgiving are valuable tools for enriching our lives with each other and broadening our own personal experience so that we can lead lives of hope, love, and joy.

It is easier to forgive an enemy than to forgive a friend.

—WILLIAM BLAKE